IN THE HOUSE OF THE JUDGE

Books by Dave Smith

POETRY

In the House of the Judge
Homage to Edgar Allan Poe
Dream Flights
Goshawk, Antelope
Cumberland Station
The Fisherman's Whore
Mean Rufus Throw Down

LIMITED EDITIONS

Blue Spruce
In Dark, Sudden with Light
Drunks
Bull Island

CRITICISM

The Pure Clear Word: Essays on the Poetry of James Wright

FICTION

Onliness
Southern Delights

IN
THE HOUSE
OF
THE JUDGE

DAVE SMITH

HARPER & ROW, PUBLISHERS, New York
Cambridge, Philadelphia, San Francisco, London
1817 *Mexico City, São Paulo, Sydney*

Some of the poems in this collection appeared originally in *Antaeus, Atlanta Magazine, Black Warrior Review, Canto, Crazy Horse, Memphis State Review, New England Review, Ploughshares, Prairie Schooner, Quarterly West, Seattle Review, Tendril,* and *Virginia Quarterly Review.*

"Outside Martins Ferry, Ohio," and "Jogging in the Parlor, Remembering a Summer Moment During Snow Squalls" appeared originally in *The Nation* in 1982.

"Photographic Plate, Partly Spidered, Hampton Roads, Virginia, with Model T Ford Mid-Channel," "Of Oystermen, Workboats," "Turn-of-the-Century House," "Your Christmas Present," "House-Movers," "Commute," "In the House of the Judge," and "False Spring: Late Snow" appeared originally in *The New Yorker* in 1981, 1982.

"Mosquito Biting" appeared originally in *Partisan Review,* vol. L, no. 1, 1983.

"Rainy Day: Last Run" and "Waking in the Endless Mountains" appeared originally in *Poetry* in 1982.

FIRST EDITION

Designer: Sidney Feinberg

Library of Congress Cataloging in Publication Data

Smith, Dave, date
    In the house of the judge.

    (Harper colophon books)
    I. Title.
PS3569.M517315   1983   811'.54   82–48134
ISBN 0-06-015075-0   83 84 85 86 87 10 9 8 7 6 5 4 3 2 1
ISBN 0-06-091022-4 (pbk.)   83 84 85 86 87 10 9 8 7 6 5 4 3 2 1

This book is dedicated to Sue Smith, who
made it possible for me to live in her
father's house in Montrose, Pennsylvania.

Contents

Behold, now the day has waned toward evening; pray tarry all night. Behold, the day draws to its close; lodge here and let your heart be merry; and tomorrow you shall arise early in the morning for your journey, and go home.

Judges 19:9

PART I

Building Houses

Through quail scattered and dawn mists in Virginia,
along the fallen trunk of cherry framing
the Dismal Swamp, we came, father and son,
into the hammered place, stepping
from a weir of brambles beside
the garden of the bent woman
whose red fingers hung
her still boiling housedress. Her eyes flare

again on me with her ammonia that all night
seeps inside my head. I stand looking
homeward under a tide of stars
for ground our house rose on,
but only her hawk-whistle
of rage returns to me,
and the flight of families.
Tonight I have tried to tell
children the history of our house.
Now they sleep. Now the flood moon
spins me to a skirt of light almost dancing.

★

We went all summer to watch, father measuring the cut
that oozed its indelible syrup of pine,
me sometimes holding the tape's tip,
leaning away, longing to be one
of the shining shadows
who climbed to jam in the gold rafters.

Beanfields uncoiled and snapped with September heat.
In that light I stood with the steady gaze
of a quail's eye. Carpenters
in midair sang while
out of the field a black son
ran, tall, who now runs
unfaced in my mind until planks
crack like a Saturday night special, and he sinks.

Our father's house went up fast, floored, timbered, roofless,
a cage of hardwood laborers hacked names in.
I try to measure my mouth as they did
to make a bird's homecoming call,
but from nail's ring and saw's talk,
there is summoned only this
grandmotherly other from her curtained nest.

★

The fathers have gone off in their trucks, the black
boy and I, lunch wolfed, put on a stone
the .22 shell I stole for myself.
From a rafter I drop the brick,
that small sudden backfire.
Through the sun's beams we run,
harried by that long dead neighbor's outswooping.

Returned from a rutted road kept by stars, I find
those indicting faces, and a wounded crone,
hand wrapped in lace, roseate,
who bursts through mounds of clay
bulldozed by the dead; she claws
us from dogwood where, hiding,
we huddle in fear and hiss our innocence.

His father's belt that whined at the split skin
of his back was brown as her nails, but I
said no word, unwhipped, clinging
to my place while she stripped
her kerchief from palm's meat.
Under naked timbers all fell and circled her,
cooing, it seemed, at some beauty I did not understand.

★

Night's blue would come over the earth, fire would leap
from the trashed wood where we hovered,
laughed, silhouettes, trying now
to joke off bad luck that came
on us with smoke's odor—the tick
and snap of embers unhousing my dream
of home, her raw hand and the hole of her
gullet screeching, ". . . you nigger sons of bitches git. . . ."

Late, I see stars burn at a forgotten window alive
in my brain and I walk near the freeway
where the faceless roar ahead.
I watch their tracers of light.
I think of the convergent dead
who prayed us peacefully asleep.
When I asked my father where she meant,
his bald head, in moonlight shining, furrowed
like the treeless ground I walk, lowered to say, "Nowhere."

★

Crone, mother of shades, where did you send them? Tell me
what house built of blue worksong and truth
casts its undying light of forgiveness.
I want to go there, son and father.
Shriek again, for traffic's howl
admits me to stand before you
remembering all, palms spread.
The city of men cracks around me.
I know what hope bears, the unbuilt,
that dream of grace raging—
but where are the builders
who nail the dark and the light,
who rose freed, singing together?
Where is our home, our sorrow and love?

PART II

Photographic Plate, Partly Spidered, Hampton Roads, Virginia, with Model T Ford Mid-Channel

No one alive has seen such ice but the five-mile floor
of water so clenched itself salt broke down.
Among us even the age-wearied would not dream
you might walk the Chesapeake Bay
and look unafraid on its lucid darkness,

and the fathers of fathers, boatwrights, sailors of all
waters, never guessed this stuttering toy
might take them so far. But someone,
joking maybe, has rolled a small house
on perilous wheels down the banks
of the James, gunned it forward
for skids, runs, circles, a day
of such joyous noise the dead
seemed to have risen, so many
great-booted and black-coated are out there.

We cannot tell what they think, or if they find themselves
dancing on the road where no road ever was,
though there are long skirts, a few
thick-waisted grandmothers, even
a scatter of children cast about.
All of them are facing Norfolk,
where ships doze like unimaginable
beasts the sea has given to the dreams of men.

The Model T is small, black, plain, and appears
cornered like something risen through ice.
Hands reach in the hazed air
but do not touch what must be
chugging in a kind of terror.
The plate is dotted far and near.
Seagulls? Stains? Some mistake of glass?
And do these faces only look averted, cast down?

Among these is the one who will breed us, having crossed
a whiteness he will not speak about even to her
whose skirts he will shake us from.
But now gears spin inside him,
wheels, a future of machines. One day
he will tell my father he walked on water . . .
sick, chugging for breath, shunned as crazy,
who I remember by the habitual odor of gasoline.
When he died my father said he was too frightened to live.

Under the ice where they walk the dark is enormous.
All day I watch the backs turned away for the one face
that is mine, that is going to wheel at me the secrets of many.

Of Oystermen, Workboats

The wide, white, wing-boned washboards of twenty
footers, sloped, ridged to hold
a man's tongs and stride,
                          the good stance
to scrape deep with a motion like big applause,
plunging the teeth true beyond the known
mounds of the dead, the current carried
cloisters of murk,
                   miracles that bloom
luminous and unseen, sweet things to be
brought up, bejeweled, culled from husks,

as oystermen like odd angels glide far off enough
to keep a wake gentle as shirts on a line,
red baseball caps dipping like bloodied
heads upright, the clawed hand slapped
at the air in salute,
                      those washboards that splinter
the sun on tongs downlaid, on tines humming,

those womb-hulls harbored flank to flank at dusk
until the white-robed priest of the moon
stands tall to the sea's spume-pour
in nostrils
            of the men who sway from heel to heel,

the season come again, the socketed gray
of their eyes outward,
forearms naked past longjohns,
the salted breast-beaters at first light

lined up, ready to fly.

Sea Owl

Unlike the hawk he has no dream of height,
his shadow is what he cannot remember.
In the wide and unlit room of the night
he waits. It is always December,

with the floor of the pines full of silver.
His toys move but his claws go tight
as soundlessly he descends the stair.
Nothing knows his cradle, where the white

drone of the day hides him. The flesh-bright
ribbons tear in his grip. He dismembers
the shore's secrets. The iron spike
of the sun is all he remembers.

Boat Building at Midnight

Wind high in the spruce, like a keel's hiss, a black leaning
around this stillness, and he has gone far out
in his head, skidding beyond the least
light's outwhirl except the glow he hangs in,

breath spilling away the midges of wood to leave him
in the surf of the *sweep, sweep* his hands make
for the house of the uncreated to sail him,
forger of all here, farther than he has ever been.

Already the rib planks sawed rawly are lying pale,
slightly pelvic, and that is not sap seeping
but the salt beads of sweat sprayed down
from his dream's drifting forehead. The hand,

long gnarled, uncramps with each stroke of the plane,
faithfully coming, coming, the lathe of breath
from hidden grain lifting a path that loops
uphill above a shore he has never once stepped.

Gusts test his roof and these quicken his making.
His boots slowly fill with the starred gold
dust he stands in, turning his body
furred as a warrior's beside the first tree honed.

Around him every edge softens, lushly dusted, and he sees
the ridged faces of the sleeping, as if dead, pared
smooth as the wood of his hands. He hears green
leaping from the ever-fragrant shroud of spruce at the spine

of his moon-silvered roof, feels it, and smells the earth
the wind sends. He bears on, blistering himself,
splitting his skin to its first pink, an idea
grown bright in his head as the flick of fish

up the narrowed channel of his spine. Holding wood hard,
claiming that seed spun out of the night, formed
by what he is forming, he begins to sing
as the young do, heartlessly, without words,

breathing deep the dust and dirt, tasting salt at his lips.
The blue, flickering workshop light bathes him,
splashes the spruce roots in the yard,
pools and laps, fathomless, at stoops of the houses.

Drudge Crabber

From the workboat plowing
all day the shallow bar
there is lunar white
and nightwoven grass
and the wake's boil
of the crab cage.
It harrows and tosses
the seed, the ghost jelly.
One line, outflown, taut,
controls everything.
When he hauls, his teeth
break bright in the sun.
The cull board gathers.
There is green gone livid
now, flesh loops, dancing,
and the chattering crabs
on their white bellies
locked arm in arm.
How does he choose
among all that huddled,
whose hands pitilessly
scrape away the unwanted?
After each of his heapings,
the ring of outriding chain
echoes his ancient wish.
Ocean and planet obey him.
He has always done this.

Dry Ice

When I woke my tongue was changed, graceless,
its pitched, easy speech gone.
Inside my skin, a quickness
slowed, swelled, turned me
thorny as a thing on a branch.

My child's eye held itself wide open, black
under lazy lids, taking in the whole
schoolroom, shelves of books,
the charted signs, powers
blank as the faces of young chemists,
while I lay dreaming apart from them, fallen

on tile like a cold progression of the facts.
Around me they dawdled and marveled
as the steaming ball shrank
to the size of a tabled planet
something had left spinning
when it fled a breathless room.

I had been told of fire in this ice, but not
how to know what it knew, words only
that I put in my mouth to feel
without warning the hard step
of beasts that could shake me
loose from the little I clung to: now

the unsketched night dropped around me.
Then the pale breathers of the day
came near and leaned close to know
the sizzle and lick of meat
I was. Whirling cubes, starred
with numbers, crackled where walls end.

Letters boiled darkly to mouths of caves.
A voice hived hard in my head.
Brightly, an old teacher lay
down the blade of his hand.
I fell to a dream, a deep
whose silence taught me to howl.

When I woke on the stone floor the hovering
spoor of my kind shocked me.
Speak, speak, they cried. Long
I watched that wave-light
lapping glass jars on the shelves.
In stilled rows the famous dead floated

until I knew myself bearing their one word.
It lay in my mouth like the sun.
With knowledge I labored to rise,
to live, afraid, doomed
by that fire I had tasted, that ice
no tongue can hold to or hold back from.

Running Back

Much of what is seen is best avoided.
I squint sometimes, sometimes I go slant.
In the nature of things, inevitably,
the tackle looms, second zero
to left and right in the black and white
skull sessions. These are human dreams,
our frail approximations of reality,
becoming facts we know, or will know.

When I collide with them I begin to think
how the sportscasters will write it up,
a day of carnage, the red claw of fate,
defeat in the fourth stanza, a joke
whose ending is "You had to be there."
I've seen lips squeezed grape-like,
my own teeth litter the turf,
a string of pearls like years
cast at the feet of pale cheerleaders.

My history is that blurred chalk I see
badly after each performance. The caged
face remains, sighted over the rear
of the pigskin where I squint.
Squint or not, that's what's ahead.
Coaches with theories from Ivy League
to Midwest Renaissance will swear
the heart's given, it's all in the feet. . . .

like John Keats, say, cutting at the ode.
Some are blunter. *This is a football.*
You don't have no idea but it! Hold
on tight, don't think! I don't think

lips and teeth mean the same to them,
who see the field sideways and scream
in a jargon remotely perfect as code.
I'm paid to crack a rock that growls.

Knuckles on what used to be soothing dirt,
I stare into a line of butts and see,
beyond, that face. It talks and hurts;
therefore, I try to run artfully
behind the abstract backs of blockers,
oblique, numbered, at zero's middle.
I don't have to look for what will be
there, dark, calling incomprehensibly.

Snake: A Family Tale

Corn pale in the ashen fields, matured, near
dead according to my aunt, but nothing
I knew, being from the city.

My uncle in the late light of his side porch
told me stories of snakes in the rows,
darkness in darkness hiding.

Walking that day there was the hiss, the slick edge
of tassel against my cheek, my crying out.
Now there is wood smoke and Fall
returns his giggle when I said

"It ain't funny, dammit!"
His mouth opened, surprised, a black loop...
whatever his dusted lips might have said
less than the heap and skid of clouds I watch.

We passed the corn safe, entered pine, and he,
for God's sake, crossed himself and broke
in a downfield zigzag through
the trees' cathedral,

until his feet far ahead were going silent, trackless
as an assassin's on needles and in my head
is now only that *whoosh, whoosh* ...

("Wait! Where are we going?")

and this gliding over the needle crack of sidewalks,
him dropping out of sight, gone in a hole,
the terror in me crying, "Don't!"

when his black cropped head pops up, shining in sunlight:
Slide down here, boy!

Uncle, family fullback, the whipping hiss
of traffic I walk in makes me see
us gulleyed, breathing invisibly
the stone stupor of that creek
where I can't stop asking,
"Where are we going now?"

Your age this year, I see your hand filled with silver
the sun blinks from: it barks, the jumpy smoke
of the pistol drifts, and I float back
to the summer of your leave, Korea,
that gaudy, bedragoned jacket
you left me, green as new hay.
Years later, to some girl, I'll whisper, "All I have."

You ever take a hike, boy? I mean a long one?

For miles we hiked to find no more than a creek's ghost,
a pool clear and blue as August. Then shirt
flapping, shoes off, you pointed: it

pulsed from a vein in rocks, only the palm-broad head
riding the water, that went nearly off
with your first echoing blast.

Inside song and in the timeless shade of a black spruce
I hang as you circle and cock and shoot.
The pieces of meat bob, then sink,
turning the blue to dusk
I will swim in when the future
drops you off in a flag-clad box.

Wood smoke that day coiled from home's cookstove as you
tickled me back through the field, your life's
war for the great words striking
me deep as the green of that world.

There was a dream in my head all night, a black joining
that sent me breathless and screaming to you.

On the porch you held me as pines scraped
like the boots of men, a soldier's
half-curse making me pray
your words to be brave and speak true.

Dusk flares again and you are singing with my father,
loading my bags: a handful of .22 shells, the skin
of an ancient snake, transparent as words
we sang over wine and sweet corn, all
you could give a boy. I say them
as we dance crack-the-whip
in the black yard. I am
the tag-end, the last
of that family gone
crazy for happiness.

But what are these words that weave us through corn
except hope's unbearable sting?
They coil out of me to remember a black
thickness flickering in the sun,
a family of cars, low sobs,
the way you come home.

Can you see me standing still inside your lost silk
where moonlight flows like life's one
word in the great snake that is
all over my back? I swear
to strike only for love,
praying for the deadliest speech
to join all things in that joy
the family is—flickering,
unkillable as the sun, the sheathed green.

Smithfield Ham

Aged, bittersweet, in salt crusted, the pink meat
lined with the sun's flare, fissured
as a working man's skin at hat level,
I see far back the flesh fall
as the honed knife goes
through to the plate, the lost
voice saying "... it cuts easy as butter...."

Brown sugar and grease tries to hold itself
still beneath the sawed knee's white.
Around the table the clatter of china
kept in the highboy echoes,
children squeal in a near room.

The hand sawing is grandfather's, knuckled,
steadily starting each naked plate
heaped when it ends. Mine
waits shyly to receive
under the tall ceiling
all aunts, uncles have gathered to hold.

My shirt white as the creased linen, I shine
before the wedge of cherry pie, coffee
black as the sugarless future.
My mother, proud in his glance,
whispers he has called for me and for ham.

Tonight I come back to eat in that house the sliced
muscle that fills me with an old thirst.
With each swallow, unslaked, I feel
his hand fall more upon mine,
that odd endless blessing

I cannot say the name of . . .
it comes again with her family
tale, the dead recalled, Depression,
the jobless, china sold, low sobs, sickness.

Chewing, I ask how he is. Close your mouth, she says.
This time, if he saw me, maybe he'd remember
himself, who thanklessly carved us
that cured meat. The Home has to
let us in, we've paid, maybe we
have to go. I gnaw a roll
left too long on the table.
When my knife screeches the plate,
my mother shakes her head, whining like a child.

Nothing's sharp anymore, I can't help it, she says.
Almost alone, I lift the scalded coffee
steeped black and bitter.
My mouth, as if incontinent,
dribbles and surprises us.
Her face is streaked with summer
dusk where katydids drill and die.

Wanting to tell her there's always tomorrow,
I say you're sunburned, beautiful as ever,
Gardening has put the smell of dirt on her.
Like a blade, her hand touches mine.
More? she whispers. Then, ". . . you think
you'll never get enough, so sweet,
until the swelling starts, the ache . . .
it's that thirst that wants
to bust a person open late at night."
I fill my cup again, drink, nod, listen.

Outside Martins Ferry, Ohio

1

Among the ashen husks of the Japanese he longed
to be small, to rise
as the mist does
at the heart of our country,
with its one idea of burning out,
and gawked at the moon
beginning to behold
his father. From this
turnpike he walked far,
only to stand in icelight
where the poets and brothers
rocked in the rickety
porch-dark of his body.
Unashamed, he bowed
to our home, wherever that is.

2

The fragile hooves in the rain kick long
to see the tall shape he has become.
There by the fence we remember,
they stand as another country
repeats its thinning tale
along shaken barbed wire.
A wide green light
fills an old woman
who knits from an animal
the hairy beasts
a child might dream.
Somewhere off a man laughs
greatly into her heart,
that softening apple.

3

He feared himself.
He feared the carcass of silkweed
the shuttled rivers of America pipe to and pitch aside.
He feared the tall fathers in company houses
counting their slagged pennies.

He feared the Eagle's terrible wings
rhyming royal, their end.

Let him go.
Let him go from the stoop and dusk of his house,
and ours, to watch beyond the river
that easy leaping colt
on ground we cannot see,
that moon's tongue, silkweed,
dreaming him its
father and brother.

An Ode to Salt Lake City

On the occasion the Prophet, Spencer Kimball,
received a revelation from God admitting
black males to hold the Mormon priesthood

Six of them sitting along a concrete curb
like evacuees of the Sears parking lot.
Or consignment statues waiting for lawns.
All black, smudged with an elder's whiskers,
wine-darkened jeans, uniform celestial shirts.
Every eye is shaded, squinting to a slot
honed by everpresent sun. The sly yawns,
long teeth, hooked nails are the desert's dirt.

Salt Lake is western, progressive, very moral.
Such obstacles on redemption's tongue
are whisked off by polite cops with pistols
and Bibles, descendants of Smith, Young,
and General Sheridan ("The only good
indians I ever saw were dead"). Yet would
Federal money flow if these were long
gone? They may be saints, the Prophet squeals.

Money and vigilance can renovate their sins,
as grass is fattened by hosts of sprinklers.
Decreed: drinks only in hotels and only when
registered. Your angel brings a minibottle.
She won't mix. Good laws eliminate human litter.
Laws come, cops go, these outlaws whistle
back, spores we cannot shake. To you, Sirs,
a taste of the grape. We laugh. A buck each one.

Snow Owl

In snow veined with his blood and the white bruise
of a broken wing, the hiss in the mouth
salutes my hand and will have still
its pink plug of flesh.
Big as I am he would nail me
if only the legs lasted, those nubs
never made for this crawling, wings
that all night beat nowhere. He is himself. *Here,*

Here, I cluck, on my knees edging toward him,
my own mastery the deceit of words.
His eye cocks, the hinged horn
of the beak tracks and rasps,
gathers its voice, shrills,
shrieks with a wind's rage . . .
the only language given to his kind

giving now his blunt answer to a world of pain.
I cast words on his white attention
like an ice he can't escape.
At each angle his bad wing
sends a storm of snow
between us, a blind conceit,
until I leave him, beaten,
who I never abandon in this life

of going home with flecked blood and snow's feather
on me like a shape I never have had.
Through the last spit of light,
trackless and numb, I go
limping until I cannot
stand, then lean on rock.
Out of this the moon rises.

All I know is this eye
long closed, holding
the world's unsayable secrets,
lifting and beating me onward.

Ducking: After Maupassant

You blew away, feather-brained for beauty.
    Our gift is your sored blessing.

As when I was a child put away by my father
    in the seal of sleep, I passed
        under pines to an under-
belly of mists, and now I wait by our

duckpond's darkness. Here I lift my face
    and the spear-slender gun when
        the tooth-shaking shroud
of ice shall from my limbs in the sun rise

like words I have never been able to say.
    You knew my kind, and the tolling
        even in the Mallard head
that like death's loud shock could not be

driven from any room where you lodged. Soon
    flecked gold is going to be spilt
        in this place, and I am one
hunched to kill whatever will leap before

the back-rocketing daylight. I am unchanged
    by your sweet fable of fidelity
        but think of a downed hen
and the drake you sent skidding into words

above her forever. Mostly you had to hope
    Nature was not what you knew, or
        more than that syphilitic
trail you left in the streets of Paris—

but all was, in the end, exactly as all seemed.
   You lay wheezing and oozing, not
      able even to imagine a face
that, being blind, you could no longer see, and

licked the night's black crust of blood from lips.
   By daylight screamed for paper,
      pen, a useless candle, then
threw open your blank eyes wide as a whore's

legs, and let it flow. It was done at last, her
   scratching ended, the door clanked
      shut with a sound like shells
I have chambered already. In the far morning

you heard the hysteria of dogs, and the crows,
   turning them back into the dreamed
      thousands of ducks exploded
aloft that day you'd taken carriage and whore

for a cruise in the country. No one understood
   you, least of all her. Beautiful,
      she cried at the gunshot,
the gaudy cloud spiraling, and you slapped her.

How vile her cursing, yet inside you these words
   glowed, they were useful. A farm girl,
      more than you she knew blood's
unreasonable purposes. Groaning, Ah, Monsieur,

she took your thrust after thrust while the time
   crusted in your head that would seep
      out black nights later, enter
another's hands with your words, at one sitting

become everything you had to believe in or die. And
   died anyway, when done, stiffening to
      meat, and so much for Nature's
fabled fidelity. But you would not be unknown.

_____

Even now your dream draws up my barrels, wind
   sifts the thin down of my hair, and
      I think what it cost you, what
willingly you paid: the stories you tried out

whore after whore, giving them your flesh and blood
   for the last lie, for feathery dawn,

        our wordless father.

Gramercy Park Hotel

"Offering the only privately owned park
in New York City. Ask at the desk for a key."

Genteel, elegant once, the place has seen hard times
that leave the walls pocked like an actor
out of make-up. Waiters crawl in uniforms
stained from old fish, their accents
bubbling up countries far distant.
Plumbing knocks, pressure is asleep,
no one answers the phone. Surely
this is home—it has the feel
of arrival, nonchalant
guests whose babble is determined and cool.

One of them, thirteen floors up I arise, shower, shave
to a new man, and feel bravely tall
as the light that filters through
a dirt-spattered window. If they
could see me now, I think—
and see myself as a fist
uncurling after the night's
flight through dreams
slipped off like loud silks.
But what now? I stand paralyzed,

as if all that I am and have been has burned away to this
curious stranger, this dark stalk in a mirror.
A sound like my teeth on clam-grit comes.
I throw open the window to breathe.
In the dank smell of concrete,
old bricks, raw fumes,
it breaks through like narcissus,
the upthrusting will to live,
the park that opens to me
one green eye, lined with hard silver.

Then there it is, the wink, the ripple over the heart,
a small wind tilting the leaves, some gesture
I imagine rising from roots deeply buried,
a light I saw once foam and spread
in sea water where a big thing
waited, sluggish, long, to leap
and convulse the sky. Gone,
was this the same flat green?
The only horizon? As if in answer
comes a swarming cloud of minnows,

joggers, multicolored feeders that surge and flash,
hungrily pouring around the park. Is
there some death near now? Is this
why I feel my shadow leave my body
to creak down caged
in the gilded elevator
where I might burst out
luggageless and laughing
among those I will never understand?
What history, what life is here
that I would want to be running
at the Gramercy? What business have I
hailing cabs and more in this tenebrous city?

One more look down. The park shrinks, a sparse
green now more memory of woods than woods,
no bird call or bright flash. What was,
like the key kept below, a trick
of the eye, nothing I may claim.
I shield my forehead and try
to find the faithful, gleaming
Atlantic—that promise.
Behind me conversations, doors
slammed, the tick-tick of our falling.
I will not be here long, will take
a careless kiss, having no time for that key.

No Return Address

My son, gangly as the colts your family raised,
lolls around the table, then sniffs
at supper he barely eats before
he bolts to his room. He's saddled
with youth we had those boring Sundays
in church under tall pines years back.
Our girls are scattered in sleep as I
listen to the static rock surrounding
his lessons. He knows you only as
a name in the unimaginable place
where we began, a blurred idea.
I remember reading your awful scrawl.
It has got no better with time.

Five years, lumps that should have been run off
like too many potatoes, your letter names
our age, from Adidas to long laps
in therapeutic pools blue as memory,
an order of despair endured. You hiss
at treatments, sizzling rays, poison,
("...enough to kill *it,* not me ..."),
those lies, we thought, in church ...
when we thought at all. All swirls
abstract as a sermon in my head
trying to translate: you hired one
cabbie, black, to watch all night
the thing you had become, motel
like a tomb he'd help you rise from,
wife, child in one bed miles off
("If I died he'd know where to go,
what to do. I wanted them at home.")

How can I answer the news in these words?
Weather? Nights here are cold, they

horse at the windows. We're stalled,
we can't sneak out. Do you remember
your family's black Studebaker, how
heroically we jumped from Sunday school
that May night, hot-wiring it? You
clutched, ground, unclutched,
hiccuped that hundred yards
to die under the caution light
at Casteen's Pure Oil? Casteen
like a giant in all that pale light
laughing, leaving us alone to push
our way in the darkness. Why? Old
as the world, that bastard was no help.

What were we that buggy summer, thirteen?
Jesus God, I'm as far from home as you,
uselessly trotting out sleek words
to make a place real for children.
You've done the same: the same tale
lied again, you and I caroming
in your father's hearse, nearly that,
to the bootlegger's lightless shack,
dogs snarling, a creek that stank,
me cringing while you nibbled out
some bills, paid, laughed as black
as the man who howled come anytime.
We've lived this lie so long it's
how we found the world we didn't know.
In words you try to hobble how you
think it was for others, for real.
The truth is we had no fast phrases
for racy girls. We crawled by stones
in the churchyard, gagging on the hope
what filled us would pass, forgiven.
The truth is we were alone, and are.

Wasn't that what Casteen meant to teach us,
leaving us to snort those heady words
of frail courage? That black cabbie,
hiring his kindness out all night,
drove you somewhere in silence.
You were pale as a drunken boy.

He mailed your letter, not a word
of address, of home, of any fate.
He's as invented as ancient Casteen,
sailing fares across a dark place
I can't guess. How can I explain
to children all of us are thieves
he'll catch breathless and foolish
no matter where we are or what we say?
Young, we thought being alone was
Sunday's grief, a boredom unrelieved
by pews of kin. We lied to be
together and alone. Now we are.

When my father died you brought me the news.
Seventeen, huddled with a girl, I howled
at Jerry Lewis on the screen until
your blinking flashlight hooked me.
A shadow, you didn't speak. I don't
hear anything you said even now, but
see that field of bobbing heads, all
wide-mouthed, pale, laughing as you
lead me through them. It's a Sunday
in May and we gallop over roads
I should know but don't. It rained,
and now rains here. I sit alone again.
I'm my father's age, diabetic, going
blind, and your letter doesn't say
where you are. How can I reach you?
I go upstairs. Static fills a boy's room.

I snap it off. But rain gone to snow rasps
the window and I stand shadowing him,
wordless. I've been watching local news,
the usual drunks, assaults, inexplicably
missing persons, a wash of words. Fronts
are moving in, bad days, and the man
advises us to stay home if we can.
If not, he says, keep shovels handy
for deep drifts, maybe flares, and a friend.
Reruns follow, anthems, and a luffing flag.
My boy, thirteen, breathes evenly, dreams,
his homework, as always, not yet done.

What should I say? I kiss his cool head,
then for a while I watch a streetlight.
From here I can see it pulse in wind,
a message I don't understand. On and off.

PART III

Love Blows in the Spring

How speak of this? How make those words
　　　as smoke from the mouth, soft,
　rises and not entirely is a silence
but enough so our sighs, like wings, may

spread and be something the face can keep.
　　　A Cardinal tongues his red
　berry until it draws up perfected
to throb like an eye where no eye is.

Come down, then, come on, and I will lie
　　　clotted, stilled, a horizon,
　as your eyebrows, snowed, blink back
and the black spruce of the witchy night

shall weld us rib and rib to the ice of her
　　　springing spine. Let the red
　bird drink of the split mud's fetch,
dipping his bone at the day's slick slit

long and long draining himself for the joy.
　　　Let him be swelled as now I am
　to sing, when first I wake, the brutal
tune of more, more while the crone scratches

free of her fleas and the white day glides.
　　　If we look, we shall not speak.
　If speak, we shall see berries fall.
When berries have fallen, the season is winged.

To Celia, Beyond the Yachts

May Day, beyond the shoal, spools the fishermen
  loose under striped thrust of the lighthouse.
    Flags and lines troll the gusts of sea wind and I

sit on the black hood of my car, shirtless, shivering,
  sun thin, the rock music blaring my battery dead.
    Like Breughel's plowman that pale, ordinary day,

we could have seen the cradling dunes scorn us. Returned,
  I look for the seahawk above his shadow and watch
    his silver fish drop, glinting back to the channel.

He makes no cry at the raucous air. Cape Charles holds
  the sun in its deep thighs. Close in, the white
    abrasions of hulls do not move. The sinkered rods

stay hooked to the dark. Once, grinding your life in
  your teeth, we lay naked here, then you leaped to lie
    in that sea. I hear the motors again, the loud yells,

as if you had fallen from the sky, sleek, sudden, dreamed.
  Crude as a fishwife but childish at men's hands, you
    wake again in my remembering and sob and rake my face,

livid, a last breath. Longing is only nightmare's
  dream of time. Whatever chance we have to be healed
    must be a channel we cannot fathom. Your letters

floated back, dots so far apart a child couldn't link
  them, closer, a daily line, then only absence, white
    paper in my hands where your breasts stirred, drifted

as these yachts that shimmer along the sheet of the Cape.
No gulls dive for entrails. Gold grit lined your mouth.
I'm freezing. I hook up my throat to the sun and see

the hawk ride out. I want to know what his eye knows,
why love made you leap down a turning tide, a looping
rise and fall of scream I hear you make with him.

I look at the far faces of men who could love you enough
if you sang up out of the sea . . . each is one I am,
skidding line in the wake, paying out a huge hunger.

Snapshot of a Crab-Picker Among Barrels Spilling Over, Apparently at the End of Her Shift

Clacking and gouging when huddled,
these well-armored warriors
sweat in dimmed sun and scuttle
in the small space each has.
Long arms salute liegelords just
passed, shadows, the honed meat
hard under those scarred helmets.
Sea-promised they come and wait,
season and season always the same.

Near these the squat houses, lights
burled, where a girl will go step
athwart the sharp road of shells
down to a shadow who's dug in
his feathery heels and hovers now
as the liquid night swells, lifts
her with first mooncrest to ride
upon him until she will lie
pale in the frost's breath, spent
flesh the white flaky treasure
these homebound, wordless, breed.

What they offer she will offer,
with sea-smell on her hands
that clean and cradle and keep
against the dull day hours
of simple dreams: hunger, flight,
the tidal force like despair
that under moons shall idle,
singing for the armorless one
love she smiles at, a taste,
faint, she cannot flee ever,
of legions at her lips biting.

Sunday Morning: Celia's Father

The man stops in his labor to sweep at his forehead
with a glove stiffened to a claw, leaves
at his feet not yet lit but already
smoldering with the light of death.

I see him take off his hat to the passing children,
the bright, uncomprehending belief on them,
leaving their arms well laden
with hymnbooks and unalterable words.

For him what is real is dying Summer, the hot clutter
that comes and weaves in the maples
now gone to more than gold . . .
but when a few small faces

fold against the unexpected rattling gusts, tears
whipped along the edges of their eyes,
often he finds himself kneeling,
scratching with stiffened arms

to reclaim each unfired cheek of green wind remembers
and skids past the circle of his keeping.
Often I see him pause and rise,
tall, as if a chill digs in.

Some mornings he calls the strange children to him.
They gather fists of pine cones and feed
his fire. He knows this is forbidden,
but the cold, hours of leaves overwhelm him.

When that yellow smoke rises like a daughter's hair,
he rakes, dances with small caps and coats.
They ride him like an old stick risen
and he beats them into laughter, helplessly.

Mosquito Biting

Nosing the oiled gravel that gleams like passion
left years back under the yellow caution
light hung across from the cemetery
at Churchland Highway and Emmaus Road,
a colorless and rock-throbbing Chevrolet
stops in the dead center of midnight's glow.

Flipping a dime, the hand in the backlit door
of the Pure Oil Station, Elmer Casteen's,
halts, hovers long enough to take
the quick thrust of a single summer
bite, then spreads the small, dark stain
as the dime rings, its glimmer in my mind all

I need to hear again the laughter of that velvet
Saturday night. Around me something frail
ticks, invisible, relentless, almost
only an idea pulsed out of the darkness
not even good window screens keep out.
Honeysuckle and pine thicken my breathing

and wake me to lie naked in myself, wishing
the clock did not buck from minute to minute,
the night would go cool, enough to draw
near the one restless beside me.
Heat lightning far off shimmers like hope,
its flashed yellow on me like a deadly pallor.

I turn in my head to that time, endless as youth,
when a girl slipped from my side to stand
between two crossing headlights, an ache
of beauty I saw squat, lift, let go
her brassed water to ring like many
dimes all over the stones of the dead.

Casteen, emptied by age, your business long failed,
do you somewhere still whoop, surprised,
grabbing yourself like an old coach
for joy? The hum of that night
drones in my ear until I see
a moon float on the eyes of a girl

gilded fully for all the hunching hours we did
not think would end. Out there a boy races
home the family car, still swelling
the night with laughs, bad music,
a name softly whining inside him.
It will call, late, just as he lies down.

Where the parents sleep in memory's half-life, it
will float like a face barely speaking,
a roll of light's glimmer, not
summonable or known, leaving us again
awake to slap and claw at ourselves
for the stinging we cannot make go or stay,

until at last, rigid as stones, we rise, stand
midway between night's unpredictable pulse
and the pure deadly revelation of naked
light in our rooms. Lying as still
as I can I listen to each distant squeal.
Somewhere music rasps the moonless words

I think of those given to darkness.
I think of you, Casteen, alive
in that pure tomb of light,
sleepless, dying to know
a girl's name, slapping hard
as I, now, slap myself and wait, stung.

Vermont Cabin: Late Summer

A rainy vacation day, one far bird jittery
with no message I have learned to understand,
thick spruce sodden, everywhere wordless,
leaning at windows where water's almost
soothing heel-click through puddles is all I have
of you. Scattered daisies droop their heads
like children bored by games gone on too long.
The wadded *Times* sticks to the floor, abandoned.
I roll as if touched on Summer's rank mattress,
as if not startled: at the door my boots stand,
two long necks broken, full mouths brimming
with darkness unexpected, sourceless as the face
of love heaved from the spruce house, time
thinned by bird's rage, not redemptive but there.

Sister Celia

I was home from my war, walking April's old life, mostly
shunned by friends from my chronic youth. In truth,
they marveled I had lived, a fool, and now asked
for Speers, Wilson, a leggy redhead. What happened?
Them, the lost? they whined. *Dead. Maybe gone to Florida.*

Florida! Land of divorce and the aging child's illusion
of hope, gold skeins of skin, nothing but dreamers'
shameless delight. You know how it is, friend: unless
it's trouble you want, a dose you won't ever shake,
stick around, build a house, pay taxes and thrive. Good

advice, and maybe you'll take it as I did, but not before
I came here to lie hunched like a snow-buried bird still
able to shake loose a little. They said *misfits, ex-
cheerleaders, bums, crips, homeless fools, all there.*
You'd do what I did, maybe. I drank, got expelled,

found myself standing where I'd cracked up a Chevrolet.
I remembered in the stillest tall pines she'd eased
on me and night started tumbling until both of us
woke up in blood, the world howling with cruisers ...
oh Christ I was GI, ex, busted, back with that tune.

I think of her as the snow shivers my walls, faceless
as the dark of Saigon brothels, remember, and think
only an angel could sigh as she did *Baby, let's go
to Florida.* On a body of needles I lay, tried sleep,
thinking she's gone, must be. At dawn rose, headed

along a lane where cherry blew bright pink. Finding her
house locked, no soul in sight, I circled and knew

myself lost by the black river. Something called.
Through my head's tunnel of shade I descended
until my name came whistling out of green, her crying

Jesus, look what the cat dragged in! Why you're alive!
That ghostface drew me down into an old wood holding
an untamed horse and, friend, I lie under this roof
between snow-scat and needle of spruce and I can't
find a good word for what home is, except shit, or time

that will leave you to wait half-alive among the dead.
We are nothing but words, mostly rotten, but I tell
you her words laid me up on a stallion called Love,
big and red as a Daytona dusk, who heaved me off
and would have done worse—listen, she whacked him,

and made me get on again, cupping her hands, so I went
up like a sparrow to treetop with cat crouched near,
dug my heels deep, one fist full of hair, and roared
straight up. But what goes up, friend, must come
down, and I did, in the softest ashen green. Smiling.

Would you cry out, Lord, there can't be anything more?
You always think there's nothing more. Death is.
A certain malignant nakedness reveals itself
when you lie in the shit at the feet of love,
yet who would not dream of life with a woman gone

so far beyond words every act is a blow full of grace,
and nothing expected in return but more of the same?
You can see, sometimes, what love has in mind.
If you should wake in the pines, cracked, not dead,
certain the one beside you is, you may see what I mean.

Even a hangnail's split flesh can astonish and gag.
The platoon leader's grin, zipping up, is enough
as rain keeps drilling an earless yellow child,
or a cop, years back at the webbed windshield,
saying "these kids want to die fucking with speed"

is enough: then you walk in the world, lie down, guess
where the dream is that nightlong had loved you.

Lie still and it's easy to feel the silk sheets
the moon rides high over Daytona, her radio
numbly bristling with blues, her braceleted arm poised

above the creamy phone, red hair bucked loose, the ocean
of stars lapping her terrace . . . well, easy to feel
if your head's as empty as the universe mounting
years like snowflakes. Otherwise, words may suffice.
Try April, a hole of slithery satin, the cruelest.

That's where the ringing starts, and a lifesaver's voice,
Why, you're alive! There's almost nothing worse
to drag you from room to room like the mouse
the cat loves, those words pounding—oh Christ,
phone, ring, sing, buckle through the trees baby,

for Celia is calling you home, is calling through ice, is
screaming through the scabby weather. Listen, what
do we wait for except life's little bell zinging,
collect, the message a trip home, all the way?
Fool, before it's too late answer. Say yes. You'll pay.

PART IV

Bats

Still in sleeping bags, the promised delivery
only words as usual, our lives upside down,
we are transients lost in thirteen rooms
built by a judge who died. The landlord says
they mean no harm, the bats, and still I wake
at the shrill whistling, the flutter overhead.

I fumble to a tall window open among maples.
A car crawling a hill splashes my face with light
spread fine by mist that had been summer rain,
a sweetness that drips from black-palmed leaves.
The breeze I feel is damp, edged with mown hay,

enough to make me think the thumps and titters
I hear might be the loving pleasure of parents
unguessed, a long quarrel ended, a thrilling
touch that trails to muffled play. Slight shadows,
these are bats, residents of the house elders
built to last, the vaulted attic tall as a man

holding them hung in rows daylong like words
unuttered above the yard where children romp.
Flashlight in hand, I pass through the parlor
papered in silk for marriages the judge made,
and stand beneath the hidden door. The truth is

nothing can drive them out or contravene those
fretful, homespinning voices we cannot help
fearing as if they were the all-knowing dead.
Yet if I had one chair to stand tall enough on
I would climb with my light and shaking voice
to see whatever has lodged in their wizened eyes.

Under a room I have never seen but know, I stand
like one of the unblessed at the edge of dawn.
Smelling mold, I hear a dog's hopeless howl
and think of the stillness in the deep heads
of creatures who hang in sleep that is like love

in the children we cannot keep forever, absolute.
Each one near me unfurls a homekeeping song no
darkness or deed can kill. With them all green
from the field clings beyond each flood of light.
As if I had never been out of this room, I listen.
The sound is like rain, leaves, or sheets settling.

Turn-of-the-Century House

The leaded, wiggly glass lives in its human length
as the squall, unpredicted, slams me down late
at night to see what in the world goes on wailing.
We have no lights. Lightning like a girl's grin
stands me dead center of the parlor. It's maples.

This house has its jitters yet. It's unreconstructed,
two claw-footed bathtubs, taps that won't turn off,
doors refusing their frames. Often they danced here.
Stars on the tin roof marked the place from near hills,

settling as thick as a shawl on a woman shaken awake.
It was only memory, but she woke her sisters anyway.
They stood on linoleum. Glass rattled and pipes clanged.
A bad storm, couldn't they see that? Ice, then snow.

The maples no one could bear cutting down, dangerous now,
raked the roof. Stars turned to ice, blinding the glass.
Can you see them, trying to sing as you would? Cold
swirls at the feet, dull yellow, naked as planked maple.
Water in the pipes forms red-streaked and pearl nails.

Near the Underground Railroad

Sunday, five of us afoot in a flaming cold,
first snow crusting the maples, we release
ourselves from weeks of depressing rooms,
friendless in a new home. The village store,
a hundred years of habit, waits aloof, open.

We're led by a gift, the retriever, Caleb,
who's faithful as a dog. No yard is foreign
to him, a red wheeling shape we keep leashed
like a rumor. We're bundled, hardly ourselves,
silently buying candy, cigarettes, the news.

Furtively my boy scans the racks of magazines,
naked women, cars, seed catalogs, forbidden
worlds who'd dream lodged in this pure place?
Our southern drawls, exotic, glide old planks
as farmers watch and nod. Then up by the Pound

we shadows move. Curtains part. At naked trees
by the town's edge, a field, dogs wailing,
hidden. Caleb whines. Our girls kick at skiffs
of snow in dead grass. Except this is bone,
chips, flecks, pets the town got tired of,

debris the tall stack couldn't send skidding
back into the dark hills. They aren't men
or children, at least, I tell my snifflers.
They think there should be laws, a home
for everything. Maybe there is, now move on,

I say as we take the unmarked bed for tracks
through strangers' woods. Climbing above
the gray, sealed houses we watch the families
of honest men race carelessly to five churches.
Caleb, pulling us, shakes when bright bells ring.

Recess

I wake late, lingering in our hollowed bed.
Sun, shallow, streams over me,
little shadows darting, tease
of the maple that buds still
at the window you opened.
I close my eyes and try
to hear the yammering
robins we've watched unfurl
like dreams we cannot hold.

Last night spring rain woke us drumming
winter's clenched, resistant ground.
Lulled to drift and remember,
we lay holding each other.
You asked where birds went
in a storm's long skid.
All I knew how to say
shivered on my lips at your neck.

Abandoned, I listen to the cries of children
from a small schoolyard. The flood
of voices hides one we know
in that deluge erupting
like green along the limbs.
When they fade I imagine
the gazing out, the huddle
over desks, the years of gouging
what they cannot keep and love,
arthritic shapes of friends,
maples, simple houses, us . . .

I lie as still as the dead. Nothing sings
in the tall wood I cannot see.
Our spring is ending. Soon you
will pad in, toweled, damp.
We'll lie together, as before.
We may sleep or only talk
of what's to come: mottled
yearling birds, then adults,
heavy-bellied, then the one
left to rasp on the knobbed limbs
gone naked for the cold shut of winter.

Your Christmas Present

This year we are sending you combs of honey
from Jaynes Farm, only six hard miles
west of the village where we live.
I have run with my body that far.
All summer I approached the apple trees
burning their best green light that
had now turned gold. We wish you
the green-gone-to-gold running of joy.
We wish you to remember the nights
long and black heaving star glitter
in the bees who ran on the hours of air,
giving the gift of themselves in gold.
We have wrapped this in local spruce
that it may smell clean and stay good.
We believe the wind sings us together.
Tonight our family is standing in the yard,
under the godly blue spruce, wearing
the magical light of the star mantle.
A long window light keeps our feet gold.
If you were here you would stand with us
to face Jaynes Farm where the bees wait
to work and the apple trees shiver again
and deer crane their necks upward, ghosts
who cross and recross the human road.
On your breads, when you come to eat,
squeeze the comb between your good hands
so the gold runs out and gleams. Do not
consume the white husk or the green limbs,
else you may feel the coming of hooves
and the odd fanning of wings behind you.
Beyond this we have to advise everyone
there are gaping holes and you must
squeeze hard to think of us, filling them.

House-Movers

Steadily down highways intractable roofs creep.
Whoever chooses them seems of one mind.
Sad white, pale green, the imagined result
of a going-out-of-business operation,
their clapboard hulls betray storied weather
by flaking paint and those stone-cracked
glasses just violated. Behind them steps
hang patiently, or a family porch waits
like a quick, amazed countryman. Required,
we think, are brute shoulders, blue jaws
and knuckles that gently graze a child's
face sliding under the edge of sleep.
These do not go with the houses, moored
families who seem alive only near pastures
where their fathers have lain for years.
Empty of each worn table and broken chair
used long nights to conjure, talk, puzzle,
the houses glide over our roads like veins,
ominous as we pass them and grip our wheels.
Wherever they arrive hard ground is gouged,
papers solemnly signed, lime is laid out,
the gray bony, bite of foundations readied.
We imagine, driving sometimes behind them,
the black birdwings will start up, spiral,
a furred knob in the sumac will shudder,
clench itself down, and growl in its belly.
In a week no one will stop to feel suddenness
hunch unalterably there, like a growth,
or months after will remember what was
never so stingingly white. But shouldered
quietly at that rutted ground, our children
those first hours wait for children to pop out.

They lick their lips at the future come
as unlikely as death or birth among them.
Here, too, arrive the summoned around us,
from the tree-shrouded edges we live near,
the thick-thighed ones who pull and strike,
wielders of maul and nail and cold chain.
When we step in their tracks we become
the bare-soled children of their keeping.
We dance from their way, sidling, transfixed.
At night, our houses locked, we cannot guess
who chose how it would be. We lie under
the lipfall and spell of their hard songs.
In our heads walls ring, bow, and chant.

Commute

Driving from work along the darkly banked country
road, the river locked in its grinding teeth,
I see how yesterday's snow has ceased
to melt, has taken the clear shape
of the oncoming night into narrow ruts
where schoolbuses tomorrow will try
to huff slower, and slowly enough. Ice
glints where I am going into the heart
of my headlights and I am hard as limbs
stripped for switches, fear seeking a way

when it happens, when the cold wheel bucks back,
breaks loose, because a fool's highbeams
suddenly skid . . . then I whip around, and we
whirl like tops in the crazy country night.

How quiet those instants after, in the holding on,
enough almost to hear the river ache, the stars
whine with glacial loneliness. I am given
back alive, shocked, remembering my father's
rage at my sister's locked door, the terrible
lies she invented. Then he did not come home.

Under snow ice streaks like the defiant face
of my son, slapped, and I think of him
huddled at monsters, cartoons, his long body
already out of control, coiling, breaking
nothing but my heart . . . laughter and fear is
as sudden on him as an ice where I, now,
drive too fast, correcting, skidding at tracks

that ghost ahead, cross and recross, endlessly.
Houselights high above farms drop into fields
gone under like the river. Flying past each
I think of meat steaming on our big table,
ice in tears on the face of the man entering,
the whirled, dangerous cold around everyone,
the sweet bread broken, offered by children.

Toy Trains in the Landlord's House

Plunged into darkness, descending as if through his dream
down inside the white, austere, winterlong drafty
son of a bitch, I go as far from the courthouse
and human wreckage as he did, the Judge,
whose house we have taken to live in
like history's hulk, going past
its hugely random floors
to seek a switch and restore our light.

I enter the basement of raw stone, departing the sloped,
badly worn stairs, and arrive at his town
on mildewed tables. Tiny trains wait.
No windows intrude. The roof hangs
black-padded, starred, vision
a jury-rig of cheap mirrors.
Mountains, green and black,
rise with paper, imagined.
His tunnels abound, shops, houses,
people, dogs with feet lifted mid-step . . .

after a while I find the chair he hunched and feel
out the master switch and flip it on, amazed
that in this crypt he should appear
to turn with the light upon me,
a serious weight in his eyes,
his pallor and foreknowing of all
schedules, disasters, suddenly mine.
The coal furnace thuds just out of sight,

its roaring like a great engine, timeless and dark.
Only a dream, I whisper, this training, but wait

for a sign, my shadow drifting unaccountably
before me like one of those accused
who knew his look and felt
they were goners.

I tell myself to rise into my family's muffled steps,
flashlight still flaring from my hand, no dead
man's wish filling my head with parts
you can't order, a world turned
whole with a button pushed, yet one

spark lets me make all those years grind slowly back.
How could he not rise, abandoning restoration,
hopeless each night? Yet he kept some few
workable wheels rolling, an order
he's left me to see. In the end
who can tell this town from another?

This house, its problems, whose but ours?
The wiring's unsafe, fuses blow, circuits
corrupt irrationally . . . how can I
tell what connects to what, and why,
unless I summon the unreachable maker?

Like a great child still believing, I push buttons
and watch each tiny light glistening past.
Out of stones wedged shoulder to shoulder,
I hope, as he did, to make the homeless
dead turn the one cramped, answering
face and almost, almost I have it
when a black, racing second train
suddenly sweeps between us . . . that

mechanical wail in the faint smoke all I manage,
except the small wheels like one endless
voice crying *innocent, innocent, innocent.*
Through the dark body of the house
where I live it rounds, whistles,
and holds me midway between those
I love and those I cannot love
enough to save. Each day I feel
the homemade city rotting, weaker.

Nights come and I rise to sit like a man condemned
above my sleeping children. All the short sparks
drifting down there like the past, when
they come together in that one flash
of a word none of us here can say,
what will be left overhead, around us?
Enough, enough I say to the wind's wail,
but each day I climb down to see
what is running still, no fixer,
only a man wanting to keep
the furnace steady, the light on,
the houses whole, the dreamed voice heard.

In the House of the Judge

All of them asleep, the suspiring everywhere is audible weight
  in the winter-shadowed house where I have dreamed
    night after night and stand now trying
  to believe it is only dust, no more than vent-spew
    risen from the idiotically huffing
grandfather of a furnace in the coal room's heart of darkness.

Haven't I touched the flesh-gray sift on bookshelves, on framed
  dim photographs of ancestors, on the clotted arms
    of the banjo clock that tolls past
  all resemblance to time and clicks like a musket's
steel hammer? And every day I wipe my glasses but still it comes,
  as now, at the top of the whining stairs, I am

come to wait with my hand laid light on the moon-slicked railing.
  I hear the house-heave of sleepers, and go jittery
    with no fear I can name. I feel myself
  shaped by the mica-fine motes that once were one
    body in earth until gouged, cracked,
left tumbled apart and scarcely glowing in a draft-fanned pit.

Pipes clank and gargle like years in the ashen veins of the Judge
  when they came to his house, the dung-heeled, some
    drunk, all with stuttered pleas to free
  their young, who could make it given a chance, just
one more good chance, so they said. Impassive, in skin-folds thick
  as a lizard, he stared at the great one for a sign,

the dog across the room, who kept a wary eye and was a one-man dog.
  Overhead do the same unbearable stars yet wheel
    in bright, ubiquitous malice, and what
  am I, wiping my glasses, certain this house walks
    in nail-clicking threat, going to plead?
I look out through warped Civil War glass buffed by men now ash

where the small park he gave in civic pride lies snow-blistered.
　Sub-zero then, as now, sent fire in the opening
　　throat, but they came: tethered horses,
　striding shadows, and women who shrieked nightlong
until even gone they continued in his head. He heard them breathing.
　He painted his house a perfectly sneering white.

I stare at that snow as at a scaffold. Whose lightening footprints
　could soften my fear or say why I sniff like a
　　dog, seem to taste a skim of black air
　upsweeping the maple stairwell, and feel my hair
　　go slowly white? How many hours must
a man watch snow shift the world before he sees it is only a dream

of useless hope stamped and restamped by the ash-steps of those we
　can do no justice to except in loving them? But
　　what could he do before the raw facts
　of men cleaving flesh like boys hacking ice?
I think how he must have thought of his barking teacher of law:
There is only truth and law! He had learned the law.

But what was the truth to leave him trembling like a child in prayer?
　In late years he kept the monster by his side, two shades
　　walking alone in the ice, the nail-raker, one
　who howled without reason and clawed at the heart
　　of door after door. In the end he was known
inseparable from his beast who, it was said, kept the Judge alive.

Until he was not. Until his house emptied. Until we came who I hear
　breathing, those heads warm as banked ash under my hand
　　laid light as I have laid it on this railing.
　But are we only this upfloating and self-clinging ash
that loops freely through dark houses? Those enigmatic fissures
　I see circling the snow? Are those only the tracks

of the dog I locked out, those black steps no more than a gleaming
　ice, or the face of some brother in the dirt betrayed,
　　pleading, accusing? The moon, far off and dim,
　plays tricks with my eyes and the snow path turns dark as
a line of men marched into the earth. Whitely, my breath floats
　back at me, crying *I did not do this,* when the shuddering

courthouse clock across the square booms me back to myself. Dream's
 aftershock, the heirloom banjo starts to thud and drum
  so I turn and hustle downstairs to halt it.
  Even with my hands laid on its hands it wants to thump
   its malicious heart out, but I can do this
at least: I can hold on to help them sleep through another night.

I can sit for a while with love's ice-flickering darkness where ash
 is heavily filling my house. I can sit with my own
  nailed walker in the snow, one whistled
 under my hand without question or answer. If I sleep
he will pad the floors above the fire-pit. He will claw me awake
 to hear breathing in the still house of the Judge

        where I live.

False Spring: Late Snow

Everything in the village seemed to dance
all the dances of its kind all day long,
the whisk and pant of brooms early on,
doors slammed, dark gone to a green-gold,
the light ripeness of last leaves smoldering,
a hint of skunks on patrol, a cardinal's
ringing out the first gilt on thickened
limbs above yards, children in the streets,
from school, sweaters tied at waist, their
push and shove of shy courtship, squeals,
then the bronze houselights stepping out
from dinner, conversation low in wind

that startled me from reading, its absence
sudden as the winter's dead, the presences
who leave a house lightless, a chair empty.
Words stopped, seized like a rusted saw, as
snow buried us, eased us under, lost again.
I climbed the stairs, light-headed as a leaf,
to ride it out in dreams. I know it is
April, the blood-red bird home. A plow
grinds through winter's lie like the sun,
bumps, skitters, turns, making the earth
gleam black as the walls of a ballroom.
I think of two hand in hand, first
steps into the swirling light, music coming.

Jogging in the Parlor, Remembering a Summer
Moment During Snow Squalls

Snow in wind-shearing afternoon light swirls and at the end
of the lane's slate thickly muffled—it stands,
                                        slides, winks
into an eye, into the window looks for an instant
where I have been jogging off fat. Panting back, dizzy
with comic self-creation, I see it and stop. Or
                                        does it see?
Still it holds wet-bright as that noon of summer, then
shakes a little all over, a kind of speech, an eye-blink
fallen near me out of the memory of leaves, a dazzling imprint

of all when I was nothing. Is this only snow-spume, like words,
or something's seething? I know in the brain
                                        is a bloodless white-out
you can run back to, and wake in the dirt, in the world
of a sudden gone hair-stiff and rank. It lifted my snout
and my thick hackles. But what was it? An eye
only, shimmering? An air-rattler? And what is this
                                        but time's delight in parody?

Waking in the Endless Mountains

As if the stars were grinding audibly,
I wake scarcely an hour into the sleep
entered after watching a cottony snow slick the road.
All night words stacked in my head remembering
until I believed once again the swirled
faces of the dead were calling.

The dog at my feet growled himself awake, shook, slept.
I climbed the tall stairs to bed and fell down.
Summoned, I do not know what startles
out of me this need to walk
bareheaded in the budding village,

but only a block of darkness off a fire is dying.
Trucks with wide red lights wink and rumble.
A few men in black shrouds coil hoses
that seem to net the shining street.
Midway between this and my house

I begin to feel invisible as the whitetail buck
who, blinded by age, stumbled in this winter.
Two or three watched him until the way out
fell back in his head, leading him
where children could not help
his legs leap again in their sleep.

When I look back at the room where I lived a flaring
comes with leaf-shadows on her face
as she discovers I am gone.
The dog barks on the porch.

Nobody means to do this, to lie in the village green,
but the earth around me is cool, wet,
as if it had just been birthed.

All I want is to stand at the top of the stairs
once more, the hall light yellowing
the foreheads of my children
while I try to say softer than

the brightest star, Goodbye. Goodbye.

Rainy Day: Last Run

Suddenly the spruce limbs hang and twist
heavy with September's rain
that comes and eases the parched
hair of the Summer fields.
Under gray oceans of air
the tall, spare windows
of houses huddled a century
shrink in wet, shining resignation.

This is the last time I will run through
our village, its breath banging
at my face and chest as I labor
up cobblestones, past the young
babysitter's porch, beyond
pocked fairways, the kennel
where retrievers on hindlegs
cheer me up the killing hillcrest.

The road is familiar, its outflung loop
a song never remembered exactly,
each farmhouse and far cow
the silent bearer of a message
I go forth with, no recipient
except themselves one sweet hour
when I return, a face in green mist.

Then it breaks, big drops gathered, a wall
of water that sends me for shelter.
I wait it out like a buck wandering,
homeless, near tossing spruce,
until there is a gray stillness.
When I edge a little in the road,
I see, surprised, I have come
to the LaSalle's rotting railstation.

Lightning cracks, driving me under the dead
eaves that spill cool silver upon me.
I shiver, unable to hide longer.
Below, village lights bristle.
I smell the sour-sweet fear
from old pews, from clothes
like mine piled, abandoned
in Pennsylvania. Almost outside
my body I try to slow my breath,
to imagine a home beyond all this running.

Night-Walk, Montrose, Pennsylvania

Drunk again, Lord of moral lies, of loves, of myths,
we walk apart in the sweet night air of this village.
I take the alley to the park, salute your Yankee dead,
then you, slurring loud your name. Here we used to speak,
rehearsing our harms in puny, human chatter: growling
bellies, booze, lust, faithlessness, hope's old stink
lingering anyway, like desire, or road-slick—.
                                                                  Friend,
I stand, waiting for you in the deep-sored grass black
as eternity is if, as it seems, it is ever-wordless.
Above me stars, like croupiers, count seconds, dealing
time in no game we understand. Is all we win silence?
Now maples seem green-hooded goons. Because you are lost,
I reel, think of you at work, alone in the land's long night,
the ghostly words you scratched, loved, hated, scratched out,
                                                                     and blest.

In memoriam, J.C.G.

Leaving Town

We left the town as we had come,
shyly, as a child speaks
to a patient waiting,
hardly noticed, traffic's hush
near, and elders remembering,
shaded by stoic oaks from noon.

We whistled down the cobblestones
we walked all the hours green
bloom was going brown, then back,
past new daylilies and the pond
where a small bear stood to see
what our smaller son did fishing.

We read the names on the park plaque,
no ancestors, but Union kin, and
hailed Sue's pigeons, the white dog
walking the Judge all winter. Fire
let the siren sleep, and the farmers.
Men worked at the courthouse clock.

Rivers we crossed seemed to race us
downhill. The high moon kept ahead,
coming on, ready we knew to find
us in the rooms above the stairs
we wouldn't be clattering anymore.
We couldn't shake it, fast as we drove.

We made a game. We would count, forget,
roll ahead like the numbers of miles.
The river multiplied and stayed.
Going south, dawn was a snowy fire.
Children fishing stopped to wave.
A man in a square marched on stone.

It was too odd to explain, and wrong,
as if all we had driven away from
said not so fast, and agreed
to travel with tricks of light
or sleight of words, to be
whatever we saw the shapes we found.

Still we knew the time could not be
counted back, nor any town the same.
Daily we drove, singing roll us over,
till five lay down like the dead,
hoping we'd wake up at home,
desolate, afraid we were there.